EMMANUEL JOSEPH

The Kindness of Creativity, How Self-Compassion and Bold Choices Strengthen Communities

Copyright © 2025 by Emmanuel Joseph

All rights reserved. No part of this publication may be reproduced, stored or transmitted in any form or by any means, electronic, mechanical, photocopying, recording, scanning, or otherwise without written permission from the publisher. It is illegal to copy this book, post it to a website, or distribute it by any other means without permission.

First edition

This book was professionally typeset on Reedsy. Find out more at reedsy.com

Contents

1. Chapter 1: The Power of Self-Compassion — 1
2. Chapter 2: The Courage to Create — 3
3. Chapter 3: Embracing Diversity Through Creativity — 5
4. Chapter 4: Creative Leadership — 7
5. Chapter 5: The Role of Art in Community Building — 9
6. Chapter 6: The Healing Power of Creativity — 11
7. Chapter 7: Innovation Through Kindness — 13
8. Chapter 8: Building Resilient Communities — 15
9. Chapter 9: Nurturing Young Minds — 17
10. Chapter 10: The Intersection of Science and Creativity — 19
11. Chapter 11: Fostering Community Through Shared Stories — 21
12. Chapter 12: Creative Solutions for Sustainable Communities — 23
13. Chapter 13: The Transformative Power of Music — 25
14. Chapter 14: The Role of Technology in Creative Expression — 27
15. Chapter 15: Creative Entrepreneurship — 29
16. Chapter 16: The Impact of Community Events — 31
17. Chapter 17: The Future of Creative Communities — 33

1

Chapter 1: The Power of Self-Compassion

In the heart of every community, lies the beating pulse of individuals yearning for connection and growth. The foundation of this connection is often built upon self-compassion—a force that propels individuals to embrace their imperfections and nurture their innate creativity. When people cultivate self-compassion, they unlock a reservoir of empathy and understanding that permeates their actions, fostering a culture of kindness and cooperation. This chapter delves into the transformative power of self-compassion, exploring how it serves as the bedrock of creative expression and community building.

One of the profound effects of self-compassion is its ability to silence the inner critic, that relentless voice that undermines confidence and stifles creativity. By practicing self-compassion, individuals learn to acknowledge their mistakes and failures without harsh judgment. This gentle acceptance creates a safe space for experimentation and innovation, allowing creative ideas to flourish. As people become more compassionate towards themselves, they are more likely to take bold risks and make unconventional choices, ultimately contributing to the vibrancy and diversity of their communities.

Moreover, self-compassion fosters resilience in the face of adversity. When individuals encounter setbacks or challenges, their compassionate mindset enables them to navigate these obstacles with grace and perseverance. This resilience not only benefits their personal growth but also inspires others within the community to adopt a similar approach. The ripple effect of self-compassion extends beyond individual boundaries, encouraging a collective spirit of support and collaboration that strengthens the fabric of the community.

Finally, self-compassion paves the way for meaningful connections and authentic relationships. When people are kind to themselves, they are more likely to be kind to others, creating an environment where empathy and understanding thrive. These connections form the cornerstone of a strong community, where individuals feel valued and heard. Through self-compassion, individuals can harness their creativity to build bridges, foster unity, and create a shared sense of purpose that enriches the entire community.

2

Chapter 2: The Courage to Create

Creativity is an act of courage. It involves venturing into the unknown, taking risks, and sometimes facing criticism. The courage to create is fueled by a deep sense of self-compassion, which allows individuals to embrace vulnerability and uncertainty. This chapter explores how self-compassion empowers people to make bold choices and express their creativity, ultimately benefiting the community.

At the heart of creativity lies the willingness to experiment and fail. Self-compassion provides a safety net, encouraging individuals to take creative risks without fear of judgment or failure. When people are kind to themselves, they are more likely to pursue their passions and share their unique talents with the world. This boldness can lead to innovative solutions, artistic masterpieces, and groundbreaking discoveries that enrich the community.

Moreover, the courage to create extends beyond individual expression. It inspires collective action and collaboration, bringing diverse voices and ideas together. When people feel supported and valued, they are more likely to contribute to community projects and initiatives. This collaborative spirit fosters a sense of belonging and purpose, strengthening the bonds within the community.

Self-compassion also plays a crucial role in overcoming creative blocks and setbacks. When faced with challenges, individuals with a compassionate mindset are more likely to persevere and find new ways to approach their work. This resilience not only enhances their personal growth but also sets an example for others in the community. By demonstrating the power of self-compassion and creativity, individuals can inspire others to take bold steps and contribute to the collective well-being.

In conclusion, the courage to create is rooted in self-compassion. By embracing vulnerability and taking risks, individuals can unlock their creative potential and make meaningful contributions to their communities. This chapter highlights the importance of self-compassion in fostering a culture of creativity and collaboration, ultimately strengthening the fabric of the community.

3

Chapter 3: Embracing Diversity Through Creativity

Diversity is the heartbeat of any thriving community. It brings a wealth of perspectives, experiences, and ideas that fuel innovation and growth. Creativity, when coupled with self-compassion, can be a powerful tool for embracing and celebrating diversity. This chapter explores how creative expression fosters inclusivity and strengthens the bonds within diverse communities.

Creativity provides a platform for individuals to share their unique stories and experiences. By expressing themselves through art, music, writing, and other creative outlets, people can bridge cultural and social divides. This exchange of ideas fosters a deeper understanding and appreciation of different perspectives, enriching the community as a whole. Self-compassion plays a crucial role in this process, as it encourages individuals to approach these diverse expressions with an open mind and a compassionate heart.

Moreover, creativity can be a catalyst for social change. When individuals use their creative talents to address social issues and advocate for marginalized communities, they contribute to a more just and inclusive society. Self-compassion empowers individuals to take bold stands and challenge the status quo, knowing that their efforts are rooted in empathy and a desire for positive change. This chapter highlights the transformative power of creativity in promoting diversity and fostering a sense of belonging within the community.

In conclusion, embracing diversity through creativity requires a foundation of self-compassion. By fostering an environment where individuals feel valued and heard, communities can celebrate their differences and work together towards a common goal. This chapter underscores the importance of creative expression in building inclusive and vibrant communities.

4

Chapter 4: Creative Leadership

Leadership within communities often requires innovative thinking and the ability to inspire others. Creative leadership, rooted in self-compassion, can transform communities by fostering an environment of collaboration, trust, and shared purpose. This chapter explores how creative leaders leverage their compassion and bold choices to uplift and unite their communities.

Creative leaders understand the importance of empathy and connection. They lead by example, demonstrating self-compassion and encouraging others to do the same. By creating a culture of kindness and support, these leaders foster an environment where individuals feel safe to express their ideas and take risks. This sense of psychological safety is crucial for innovation and growth, as it empowers community members to contribute their unique perspectives and talents.

Furthermore, creative leaders embrace change and uncertainty. They recognize that bold choices are often necessary to address complex challenges and drive progress. Self-compassion enables these leaders to navigate setbacks and failures with resilience, learning from their experiences and adapting their strategies. This adaptive approach not only enhances their own effectiveness but also inspires others within the community to persevere and remain flexible in the face of adversity.

In addition to fostering a supportive environment and embracing change, creative leaders prioritize collaboration and inclusivity. They understand that diverse voices and ideas are essential for innovation and community building. By actively seeking input from all members of the community and valuing their contributions, these leaders create a sense of belonging and shared ownership. This collaborative spirit strengthens the bonds within the community and drives collective action towards common goals.

In summary, creative leadership rooted in self-compassion can transform communities by fostering collaboration, resilience, and inclusivity. By leading with empathy and boldness, creative leaders inspire others to contribute their best selves and work together towards a brighter future.

5

Chapter 5: The Role of Art in Community Building

Art has the power to transcend boundaries and bring people together. It serves as a universal language that can convey emotions, ideas, and experiences in ways that words alone cannot. This chapter explores the role of art in community building, highlighting how self-compassion and creativity can create a vibrant and inclusive environment.

Artistic expression provides individuals with a platform to share their stories and connect with others on a deeper level. Whether through visual arts, music, dance, or theater, art allows people to express their identities and experiences in unique and meaningful ways. Self-compassion plays a crucial role in this process, as it encourages individuals to embrace their vulnerabilities and share their authentic selves with the world.

Moreover, community art projects can foster a sense of unity and collaboration. When people come together to create murals, sculptures, or public performances, they build relationships and strengthen their sense of belonging. These collaborative efforts also provide opportunities for individuals to learn from one another and appreciate the diverse talents and perspectives within the community.

Art can also serve as a catalyst for social change and advocacy. Creative works that address social issues or highlight marginalized voices can inspire dialogue and action. By using art as a tool for activism, individuals can raise awareness and drive positive change within their communities. Self-compassion empowers artists to take bold stands and address challenging topics, knowing that their efforts are rooted in empathy and a desire for justice.

In conclusion, art plays a vital role in community building by fostering connection, collaboration, and social change. By embracing self-compassion and creativity, individuals can use artistic expression to strengthen the bonds within their communities and create a more inclusive and vibrant environment.

6

Chapter 6: The Healing Power of Creativity

In the face of life's challenges and adversities, creativity can be a powerful tool for healing and resilience. This chapter explores how self-compassion and creative expression can help individuals cope with difficult emotions, find meaning, and foster a sense of hope and renewal within their communities.

Creativity allows individuals to process their emotions and experiences in a safe and constructive manner. Whether through writing, painting, or other forms of artistic expression, individuals can externalize their feelings and gain a sense of clarity and perspective. Self-compassion plays a crucial role in this process, as it encourages individuals to approach their emotions with kindness and understanding. By allowing themselves to fully experience and express their feelings, individuals can begin to heal and move forward.

Moreover, creative activities can provide a sense of purpose and fulfillment during difficult times. Engaging in creative pursuits can bring joy and satisfaction, offering a welcome distraction from stress and worry. This sense of purpose can be particularly important during periods of uncertainty, helping individuals to maintain a positive outlook and stay connected to their passions and interests. Self-compassion supports this process by allowing individuals to prioritize their well-being and give themselves permission to engage in activities that bring them joy.

In addition to personal healing, creativity can foster a sense of connection and support within communities. Group art projects, creative workshops, and other collaborative activities can bring people together and provide opportunities for mutual support and understanding. These shared experiences can strengthen the bonds within the community and create a sense of solidarity and resilience. Self-compassion encourages individuals to extend empathy and kindness to others, fostering a culture of support and cooperation.

In conclusion, the healing power of creativity lies in its ability to help individuals process their emotions, find meaning, and connect with others. By embracing self-compassion and creative expression, individuals can navigate life's challenges with resilience and foster a sense of hope and renewal within their communities.

7

Chapter 7: Innovation Through Kindness

Innovation is often seen as the driving force behind progress and development. However, the role of kindness and self-compassion in fostering innovation is often overlooked. This chapter explores how a compassionate approach to creativity can lead to groundbreaking ideas and solutions that benefit the community.

Kindness creates an environment where individuals feel valued and respected, which is essential for fostering innovation. When people feel safe and supported, they are more likely to share their ideas and take creative risks. Self-compassion plays a crucial role in this process, as it encourages individuals to approach their work with curiosity and openness. By embracing a compassionate mindset, individuals can create a culture of innovation that values diverse perspectives and encourages experimentation.

Moreover, kindness can inspire collaborative innovation. When individuals work together with a shared sense of empathy and mutual respect, they can pool their talents and resources to develop innovative solutions to complex challenges. This collaborative approach not only enhances the quality of the ideas generated but also strengthens the bonds within the community. Self-compassion supports this process by fostering a sense of humility and a willingness to learn from others.

In addition to fostering collaboration, kindness can drive innovation by addressing the needs and concerns of the community. Compassionate individuals are more likely to identify and prioritize issues that impact the well-being of others. By focusing on solutions that promote social good, compassionate innovators can create positive change and improve the quality of life within their communities. This chapter highlights the importance of a compassionate approach to innovation and its potential to create lasting impact.

In summary, innovation through kindness is rooted in self-compassion and empathy. By creating an environment that values diverse perspectives and encourages collaboration, individuals can develop groundbreaking ideas that benefit the community. This chapter underscores the transformative power of kindness in fostering innovation and driving progress.

8

Chapter 8: Building Resilient Communities

Resilience is the ability to withstand and adapt to challenges and adversity. It is a crucial quality for individuals and communities alike. This chapter explores how self-compassion and creativity can foster resilience within communities, helping them to navigate difficult times and emerge stronger.

Self-compassion is a key component of resilience, as it allows individuals to approach challenges with a sense of kindness and understanding. When faced with setbacks, individuals with a compassionate mindset are more likely to view these experiences as opportunities for growth and learning. This positive outlook can help individuals to persevere and find creative solutions to problems. By fostering self-compassion, communities can build a collective resilience that enables them to navigate adversity with grace and determination.

Creativity also plays a crucial role in building resilient communities. Creative problem-solving allows individuals to think outside the box and develop innovative solutions to challenges. Whether through art, music, or other forms of expression, creativity can provide a sense of hope and inspiration during difficult times. Self-compassion supports this process by encouraging individuals to embrace their creative potential and take bold steps towards positive change.

Moreover, resilience is strengthened through connection and collaboration. When individuals come together to support one another and share their strengths, they can build a sense of solidarity and mutual trust. Creative activities and group projects can provide opportunities for individuals to connect and collaborate, fostering a sense of community and resilience. Self-compassion encourages individuals to extend empathy and kindness to others, creating a supportive environment where everyone can thrive.

In conclusion, building resilient communities requires a foundation of self-compassion and creativity. By fostering a compassionate mindset and embracing creative problem-solving, individuals can navigate adversity and emerge stronger. This chapter highlights the importance of resilience in community building and the role of self-compassion and creativity in fostering a sense of hope and renewal.

9

Chapter 9: Nurturing Young Minds

The future of any community lies in the hands of its youth. By fostering self-compassion and creativity in young minds, we can cultivate a generation of empathetic, innovative, and resilient individuals who will continue to strengthen and enrich their communities. This chapter explores the importance of nurturing self-compassion and creativity in children and adolescents and the impact it can have on the broader community.

Encouraging self-compassion in young people helps them develop a strong sense of self-worth and emotional resilience. When children learn to be kind to themselves, they are better equipped to navigate challenges and setbacks with confidence and grace. This compassionate mindset also enables them to extend empathy and kindness to others, fostering a culture of support and understanding within their peer groups. By prioritizing self-compassion, we can create a nurturing environment that promotes the emotional well-being and growth of young individuals.

Creativity plays a crucial role in the development of young minds. Engaging in creative activities allows children to explore their interests, express their emotions, and develop critical thinking skills. Whether through art, music, storytelling, or imaginative play, creativity encourages curiosity and innovation. Self-compassion supports this process by providing a safe space for children to experiment and take risks, knowing that their efforts are valued and appreciated.

Moreover, fostering creativity and self-compassion in young people can have a ripple effect on the broader community. As children grow into empathetic and innovative adults, they are more likely to contribute to the well-being and growth of their communities. By nurturing these qualities in the next generation, we can ensure a future where compassion, creativity, and collaboration are at the forefront of community building.

In conclusion, nurturing self-compassion and creativity in young minds is essential for the growth and resilience of any community. By fostering these qualities in children and adolescents, we can cultivate a generation of individuals who are equipped to navigate challenges, support one another, and contribute to the collective well-being of their communities.

10

Chapter 10: The Intersection of Science and Creativity

Science and creativity are often seen as distinct disciplines, but they share a common foundation of curiosity, innovation, and problem-solving. This chapter explores the intersection of science and creativity, highlighting how self-compassion and bold choices can drive scientific discovery and innovation that benefit the community.

At the core of scientific inquiry is the desire to understand the world and solve complex problems. Creativity plays a crucial role in this process, as it allows scientists to think outside the box and develop innovative solutions. Self-compassion supports this creative approach by encouraging scientists to embrace uncertainty and take risks. By fostering a compassionate mindset, scientists can navigate setbacks and failures with resilience, ultimately leading to groundbreaking discoveries.

Moreover, the intersection of science and creativity extends beyond individual research. Collaborative scientific endeavors often involve diverse teams of researchers with different expertise and perspectives. This diversity can lead to more innovative and comprehensive solutions to complex challenges. Self-compassion plays a key role in fostering a collaborative environment, as it encourages mutual respect and empathy among team members. By valuing each other's contributions and supporting one another, scientists can work together to achieve common goals.

In addition to driving innovation, the intersection of science and creativity can also have a positive impact on the broader community. Scientific discoveries and technological advancements can address pressing social issues, improve quality of life, and promote sustainable development. By approaching their work with self-compassion and a commitment to social good, scientists can ensure that their efforts have a meaningful and lasting impact.

In summary, the intersection of science and creativity is a powerful force for innovation and progress. By fostering self-compassion and embracing bold choices, scientists can drive discoveries that benefit the community and contribute to a brighter future. This chapter highlights the importance of a compassionate approach to scientific inquiry and the potential for creative solutions to address complex challenges.

11

Chapter 11: Fostering Community Through Shared Stories

Storytelling is a fundamental human experience that has the power to connect individuals and foster a sense of community. By sharing our stories, we can build empathy, understanding, and a shared sense of identity. This chapter explores the role of storytelling in community building and the importance of self-compassion and creativity in this process.

Stories have the ability to transcend cultural and social boundaries, providing a platform for individuals to share their unique experiences and perspectives. Through storytelling, we can find common ground and celebrate our differences, ultimately strengthening the bonds within the community. Self-compassion plays a crucial role in this process, as it encourages individuals to approach their own stories with kindness and acceptance. By embracing our own vulnerabilities and imperfections, we can share our authentic selves with others and build meaningful connections.

Creativity enhances the storytelling process by allowing individuals to express their experiences in unique and engaging ways. Whether through writing, visual arts, theater, or digital media, creative storytelling can capture the imagination and inspire empathy. Self-compassion supports this creative expression by providing a safe space for individuals to explore their emotions and share their stories without fear of judgment. By fostering a compassionate and creative environment, communities can encourage storytelling as a means of connection and growth.

Moreover, shared stories can serve as a catalyst for social change. By bringing attention to important issues and amplifying marginalized voices, storytelling can inspire action and promote a more just and inclusive society. Self-compassion empowers individuals to take bold stands and address challenging topics, knowing that their efforts are rooted in empathy and a desire for positive change.

In conclusion, storytelling is a powerful tool for community building. By fostering self-compassion and creativity, individuals can share their stories and connect with others in meaningful ways. This chapter highlights the transformative power of storytelling in fostering empathy, understanding, and a shared sense of identity within the community.

12

Chapter 12: Creative Solutions for Sustainable Communities

Sustainability is a critical concern for communities around the world. Creative solutions, rooted in self-compassion and bold choices, can help address environmental challenges and promote sustainable development. This chapter explores how individuals and communities can leverage their creativity to build a more sustainable future.

Creativity allows individuals to think outside the box and develop innovative solutions to environmental challenges. Whether through sustainable design, renewable energy, or community-driven initiatives, creative thinking can drive positive change. Self-compassion plays a crucial role in this process, as it encourages individuals to approach these challenges with empathy and a sense of responsibility. By fostering a compassionate mindset, individuals can prioritize the well-being of the planet and future generations.

Moreover, sustainable communities are often built on collaboration and collective action. Creative projects and initiatives can bring people together to work towards common goals, such as reducing waste, conserving resources, and promoting environmental awareness. Self-compassion supports this collaborative approach by fostering a sense of mutual respect and understanding. By valuing each other's contributions and working together, communities can develop sustainable solutions that benefit everyone.

In addition to promoting sustainability, creative solutions can also enhance the quality of life within communities. Green spaces, public art, and sustainable architecture can create vibrant and livable environments that support the well-being of residents. Self-compassion encourages individuals to prioritize their own well-being and that of their neighbors, creating a culture of care and stewardship.

In conclusion, creative solutions are essential for building sustainable communities. By fostering self-compassion and bold choices, individuals and communities can address environmental challenges and promote a more sustainable future. This chapter highlights the importance of creativity and collaboration in driving positive change and building resilient, sustainable communities.

13

Chapter 13: The Transformative Power of Music

Music has the power to uplift, heal, and unite people. It serves as a universal language that can transcend boundaries and foster a sense of connection and belonging. This chapter explores the transformative power of music and the role of self-compassion and creativity in its creation and impact on communities.

Music provides individuals with a means of expressing their emotions and experiences. Whether through composing, performing, or listening, music allows people to connect with their innermost feelings and share them with others. Self-compassion plays a crucial role in this process, as it encourages individuals to approach their musical expression with kindness and acceptance. By embracing their vulnerabilities and imperfections, musicians can create authentic and meaningful works that resonate with others.

Moreover, music can bring people together and foster a sense of community. Group performances, community choirs, and music festivals provide opportunities for individuals to connect and collaborate. These shared musical experiences can strengthen the bonds within the community and create a sense of unity and belonging. Self-compassion supports this collaborative approach by fostering a sense of empathy and mutual respect among participants.

In addition to its social benefits, music can also have a profound impact on mental and emotional well-being. Research has shown that music can reduce stress, alleviate anxiety, and promote relaxation. By incorporating music into their lives, individuals can enhance their overall well-being and resilience. Self-compassion encourages individuals to prioritize their mental and emotional health, creating a positive feedback loop that supports their personal growth and the well-being of the community.

In summary, the transformative power of music lies in its ability to connect, heal, and inspire. By fostering self-compassion and creativity, individuals can harness the power of music to enrich their lives and strengthen their communities. This chapter highlights the importance of musical expression in fostering a sense of connection and well-being within the community.

14

Chapter 14: The Role of Technology in Creative Expression

Technology has revolutionized the way we create, share, and experience art. It has opened up new possibilities for creative expression and collaboration, transforming the landscape of art and culture. This chapter explores the role of technology in creative expression and the importance of self-compassion and bold choices in navigating this digital age.

Technology provides individuals with a wide range of tools and platforms for creative expression. From digital art and music production to virtual reality and interactive media, technology has expanded the possibilities for artistic creation. Self-compassion plays a crucial role in this process, as it encourages individuals to embrace these new tools with curiosity and an open mind. By approaching technology with a sense of kindness and acceptance, individuals can explore its potential and push the boundaries of their creativity.

Moreover, technology has made it easier for individuals to share their work and connect with others. Social media, online galleries, and digital distribution platforms provide artists with opportunities to reach a global audience and build communities around their work. Self-compassion supports this process by encouraging individuals to share their work without fear of judgment and to value the feedback and support of their peers. By fostering a compassionate and collaborative environment, technology can create a sense of connection and belonging among artists and their audiences.

In addition to its creative potential, technology can also be a powerful tool for social change. Digital activism, online campaigns, and virtual events can raise awareness and mobilize communities around important issues. Self-compassion empowers individuals to use technology to advocate for positive change, knowing that their efforts are rooted in empathy and a desire for justice.

In conclusion, technology has transformed the landscape of creative expression, offering new possibilities for artistic creation and collaboration. By fostering self-compassion and embracing bold choices, individuals can navigate this digital age and harness the power of technology to enrich their lives and strengthen their communities.

15

Chapter 15: Creative Entrepreneurship

Entrepreneurship is a powerful driver of economic and social development. Creative entrepreneurs, fueled by self-compassion and bold choices, can transform industries, create jobs, and contribute to the well-being of their communities. This chapter explores the role of creativity and self-compassion in entrepreneurship and the impact it can have on the broader community.

Creative entrepreneurs approach their ventures with a sense of curiosity and innovation. They are willing to take risks and explore new ideas, knowing that failure is a natural part of the process. Self-compassion plays a crucial role in this process, as it encourages entrepreneurs to embrace their mistakes and learn from their experiences. By fostering a compassionate mindset, entrepreneurs can navigate the challenges of building a business with resilience and determination.

Moreover, creative entrepreneurship often involves collaboration and community engagement. Successful entrepreneurs understand the importance of building relationships and leveraging the strengths of their networks. Self-compassion supports this collaborative approach by fostering a sense of mutual respect and empathy. By valuing the contributions of others and working together, entrepreneurs can create thriving businesses that benefit the broader community.

In addition to driving economic growth, creative entrepreneurship can also have a positive impact on social and environmental issues. Social entrepreneurs, in particular, use their creative talents to address pressing challenges and create solutions that promote social good. By approaching their ventures with self-compassion and a commitment to positive change, these entrepreneurs can create lasting impact and contribute to the well-being of their communities.

In summary, creative entrepreneurship is fueled by self-compassion and bold choices. By fostering a compassionate mindset and embracing innovation, entrepreneurs can build successful ventures that contribute to economic growth and social good. This chapter highlights the transformative power of creative entrepreneurship in driving positive change and strengthening communities.

16

Chapter 16: The Impact of Community Events

Community events are powerful tools for bringing people together, fostering connections, and creating a sense of belonging. Whether it's a local festival, a community clean-up, or a neighborhood art show, these events can have a lasting impact on the well-being and unity of the community. This chapter explores the role of self-compassion and creativity in planning and participating in community events and their potential to strengthen communities.

Community events provide opportunities for individuals to connect, share their talents, and celebrate their collective identity. By fostering a spirit of collaboration and inclusivity, these events can bring people from diverse backgrounds together and create a sense of unity and belonging. Self-compassion plays a crucial role in this process, as it encourages individuals to approach these events with empathy and an open heart. By valuing the contributions of others and embracing diverse perspectives, communities can create events that are meaningful and impactful.

Creativity is also essential for planning and executing successful community events. Creative ideas can enhance the overall experience, making events more engaging and memorable. Whether it's through innovative activities, unique themes, or artistic performances, creativity can elevate the quality of community events and leave a lasting impression on participants. Self-compassion supports this process by encouraging individuals to take risks and explore new ideas, knowing that their efforts are appreciated and valued.

In addition to fostering connections and creativity, community events can also have a positive impact on the broader community. They can raise awareness about important issues, promote local businesses, and generate a sense of pride and ownership among residents. Self-compassion empowers individuals to take bold stands and advocate for positive change, knowing that their efforts are rooted in empathy and a desire for justice.

In conclusion, community events are powerful tools for building connections, fostering creativity, and promoting positive change. By embracing self-compassion and creativity, individuals can plan and participate in events that strengthen the bonds within their communities and create a sense of unity and belonging.

17

Chapter 17: The Future of Creative Communities

The future of any community lies in its ability to adapt, innovate, and thrive in an ever-changing world. By fostering self-compassion and creativity, communities can build a resilient foundation that supports growth and progress. This chapter explores the potential for creative communities to drive positive change and shape a brighter future.

Self-compassion is the cornerstone of any thriving community. It encourages individuals to approach challenges with kindness and understanding, fostering a sense of resilience and adaptability. By prioritizing self-compassion, communities can create an environment where individuals feel supported and valued, enabling them to contribute their best selves to the collective well-being.

Creativity, on the other hand, is the driving force behind innovation and progress. It allows individuals to think outside the box and develop new solutions to complex challenges. By fostering a culture of creativity, communities can harness the talents and ideas of their members to drive positive change and create a brighter future. Self-compassion supports this process by encouraging individuals to take risks and embrace their creative potential, knowing that their efforts are appreciated and valued.

Moreover, the future of creative communities lies in their ability to collaborate and connect with one another. By building strong relationships and leveraging the strengths of their networks, communities can work together towards common goals and drive collective action. Self-compassion plays a crucial role in this process, as it fosters a sense of mutual respect and empathy among community members. By valuing each other's contributions and supporting one another, communities can build a strong foundation for future growth and progress.

In summary, the future of creative communities is rooted in self-compassion and creativity. By fostering these qualities, communities can build a resilient foundation that supports growth, innovation, and positive change. This chapter highlights the importance of self-compassion and creativity in shaping a brighter future for communities around the world.

Book Description: "**The Kindness of Creativity: How Self-Compassion and Bold Choices Strengthen Communities**" explores the transformative power of self-compassion and creativity in building vibrant and resilient communities. Through 17 chapters, this book delves into the importance of kindness, empathy, and bold choices in fostering innovation, collaboration, and social change. Each chapter highlights the role of self-compassion and creativity in various aspects of community building, from nurturing young minds and fostering diversity to driving sustainable development and promoting mental well-being.

Readers will discover how self-compassion can empower individuals to embrace their vulnerabilities, take creative risks, and contribute their unique talents to the collective well-being of their communities. The book also explores the intersection of science and creativity, the impact of community events, and the future of creative communities, offering practical insights and inspiring examples of how compassion and creativity can drive positive change.

"The Kindness of Creativity" is a powerful testament to the potential of compassionate and creative communities to thrive in an ever-changing world. It is an essential read for anyone interested in building stronger, more inclusive, and more resilient communities.

www.ingramcontent.com/pod-product-compliance
Lightning Source LLC
LaVergne TN
LVHW010441070526
838199LV00066B/6134